Spiritual Satanist

Prayer Book

Spiritual Satanist Prayer Book

Infernal Reflections

Created by
Venus Satanas

Spiritual Satanist Prayer Book
Infernal Reflections

Published by Dark Path Press, USA
ISBN: 978-0-692-07205-9
https://www.SpiritualSatanist.com
© 2018 Venus Satanas / Melissa Hudson

All rights reserved. No portion of this book may be reproduced in any form without permission from the author, except as permitted by U.S. copyright law.

For permissions contact: VenusSatanas@SpiritualSatanist.com

Disclaimer: *The advice in this book does not constitute legal or medical advice; prayer is not a substitute for medical or mental health care, please seek the assistance of a professional if you are in need.*

FOR SATAN, WHO HAS GUIDED ME AS A
TRUSTED ALLY ~
AND FOR MY READERS, MAY THE FORCE OF
SATAN BE WITH YOU, ALWAYS

Contents

Preface		*xi*
Introduction		*1*
1.	*The Basics of Satanic Prayer*	7
2.	*Living Mindfully Through Spirituality*	11
3.	*Prayer is a Tool, Not a Crutch*	15
4.	*Respecting The Forces of Darkness*	21

5.	*The Spirit of Satan*	27
6.	*Satanic Prayers*	31
7.	*A Backwards Blessing*	33
8.	*Satan's Prayer*	39
9.	*A Satanic Blessing*	43
10.	*Laude Satanas*	47
11.	*The Infernal Trinity*	51
12.	*In Praise of Satan's Kingdom*	55
13.	*The Satanist's Creed*	57
14.	*Prayer of Satan's Powers*	61
15.	*Prayer of Satan's Riches*	65
16.	*Baphomet, The Source Of Creation*	67

17. *Lucifer, The Bringer Of Enlightenment* — 71

18. *Lilith, The Queen Of The Night* — 77

19. *Belial's Blessing* — 83

20. *Infernal Reflections* — 89

21. *Hymn To Satan* — 91

22. *Lucifer in Starlight* — 107

23. *The Lady Lilith* — 113

Bibliography & Notes — 119

Image Credits — 127

About The Author — 131

Preface

I created my *Spiritual Satanist Prayer Book: Infernal Reflections* for those who seek to have a spiritual relationship with Satan. While the symbolism of Satan is inspiring, becoming closer to Satan as a personal god is a goal for many. Prayer may help you to achieve this.

My name is Venus Satanas, and I came to discover Satanism in 1992. I created a

Preface

pact with Satan that same year seeking to work in Satan's service. The internet wasn't as popular in the early 90's, and we got most of our knowledge about Satanism through books and experimentation. By the time 2004 came around things had changed, and I decided to start writing about my experiences and knowledge in Satanism at my website.

I came to write this book when I discovered that my Satanic Prayers page at my website was one of the most popular pages. People are seeking spiritual inspiration, and they want to reach out to Satan through prayer. There are many variants of the 'Satanic Bible' available today, but rarely any books that deal with Satanic prayer as this book has done.

I realize that prayer and spirituality doesn't always have to happen in the ritual room. The pocket-sized edition of this book makes it easy to take with you wherever you go. After all, many of us live in a world where carrying around a book on Satanism can make you seem obvious.

With this pocket-sized edition, you can easily travel with this book, read it while on a break, or use it whenever or wherever you feel the need to be close to Satan's infernal powers. In a moment of doubt, or when you need some inspiration, just reach out – Satan is always there for you.

Preface

I am hoping that my *Spiritual Satanist Prayer Book: Infernal Reflections* will help you to experience the force of Satan in your life. I created many of the prayers in this book, and the poetry is sourced from history and popular culture. Both are intended to provide to you motivation and inspiration in the ways of Satan.

It is my hope that this prayer book can help you to become enlightened in the ways of Satan and other left hand path demons and deities. May the gates of the infernal realm be opened to greet you as kin!

Introduction

As a Spiritual Satanist, have you ever felt that there should be more to Satanism than just reading or talking about Satanism? There is something more that you can do. Daily prayer or spiritual reflection can help you to feel more complete. Prayer or spiritual reflection gives you something concrete you can use right now in your life. Satanic devo-

Introduction

tional prayer can be a useful tool in your spiritual journey in Satanism.

For Spiritual Satanists, prayer can help to connect you with the force of Satan. Prayer allows you to have a personal relationship with Satan that you can work on every day, both in the ritual room, and outside of ritual work.

Anyone with a sincere desire to get closer to Satan can use prayer. All it takes is a heartfelt motivation to reach out to those dark forces and make it a part of you. Prayer and reflection on Satan and his infernal realm can help you These prayers and poems for Satan can help you in your journey.

Spiritual Satanism doesn't require you to use prayer. But, in order to take advantage of what Spiritual Satanism offers, prayer is a useful tool to help guide you. Know that prayers to Satan are so much more than just a means to obtain what you want. When prayers are offered to Satan, it is not just said with words; prayer is within the heart as well. Prayer is a two way street, a form of communication with the spiritually divine.

Prayer can open the gates. Mindful prayer can be used to strengthen your bond with Satan. It can be used to give you personal strength or when you are seeking reassurance or comfort. Prayer is used to give you clarity in a situation or to receive guidance. You can use prayer anytime you feel it is necessary.

If daily devotional prayer interests you,

Introduction

then use prayer during a moment when you have time alone to be with Satan. In this prayer you align yourself with the forces of Satan, Lucifer, Belial, and Lilith. You can begin each day with a mindful presence if you use daily prayer. Prayer can bring you clarity by allowing you to calm and focus your mind. In that moment you are receptive to new ideas and opportunities. The act of reaching out through a prayer is a spiritual tool that can help you in your time of need.

HOW TO USE THIS BOOK

The first section of this book offers common prayers that you can use either on a daily basis, to start out your day, or before or after ritual. Some prayers, like the prayer for money are useful to enhance your spell work. The second section of this book offers spiritual reflections on Satan, Lilith and other demons through poetry. This book will give you spiritual inspiration for your everyday life as a Satanist.

1

The Basics of Satanic Prayer

How do you pray to Satan? Prayer is a spiritual act that connects you to a force greater than yourself. Prayer can seem mysterious because you are sending your heartfelt message out there to the universe, hoping that Satan will listen. But, prayer doesn't have to seem like a

The Basics Of Satanic Prayer

mystery. Prayer can be a useful basic spiritual tool to help you to connect with the force of Satan.

Prayer connects you with the force of Satan, where you are guided by Satan's power. The act of prayer brings you comfort in times of need. Prayer will focus your mind and bring you clarity. Prayer gives you a reason to stay true to your path and yourself. Also, prayer can help you to feel closer to Satan.

The basics of Satanic prayer are simple; you have to say the words of your prayer not just with your mind but in your heart as well. You have to know that when you pray to Satan, you are communicating with those ancient forces on a spiritual level, rather than speaking at them. When you are sincere Satan will know what is in your heart.

Prayer is a form of magic. This magic, known as theurgy, allows you to work with forces greater than yourself. With theurgy, you are calling out to deities and asking for their assistance. It is no different from casting a spell, but with prayer you are employing divine or spiritual assistance to help you.

You should be aware that while all things are possible with the magic of prayer, not all things are probable. It helps to be reasonable with your request during prayer. Prayer is not an excuse for inaction. Use prayer to supplement and compliment what you achieve in the material world.

The Basics Of Satanic Prayer

Whether prayer is a part of your daily routine, or you use it for special occasions, use this time to spiritually connect with Satan in your own way. Open your heart to communication with Satan and you will soon see the benefits of being in spiritual union with the force of Satan.

2

Living Mindfully Through Spirituality

Prayer is also a form of invocation. When you use prayer to call upon Satan, you are reaching out to that spiritual energy and connecting with it. But so many of us just go through life without living mindfully. To live mindfully in Satanism you have to have a structured environment. A daily prayer enables you to start out your day the right way, with the right mindset. To live through Satan's works you must enable yourself to live through Satan's words.

Living mindfully enables you to see the good things that Satan brings into your life, enabling you to live through the spiritual undercurrent that Satanism offers you. This undercurrent is always there, but only those who chose to live mindfully can realize it's potential and see for themselves how it influences your life. This is the secret to spiritual experience.

For those who are new to spirituality, it might seem that prayers are just empty words. You should set aside your expectations instead and just let things happen for you. High expectations and false hopes only lead to disappointment and frustration. Spirituality should not be frustrating. If anything, it is liberating, allowing you to live a fuller life.

In simple terms, spirituality is different than religion. While religion dictates to us how we should feel, spirituality lets us feel it on our own terms, in a personal way. Religion provides the answers, while spirituality allows us to ask the questions. In its most basic sense, spirituality allows us to know and experience that our lives have a meaningful purpose – that we are material humans having a spiritual experience.

We have a physical body, but there is more to life than that. Spirituality allows you to reach out to what is already there, but hidden to those without the desire to fully experience life. Satan, in its simplest terms is the material world, thus we say that Satan 'rules the earth', or represents the material world. But there is a spirit or energy contained within all things, and prayer (and ritual, and magic, divination and meditation) and numerous other spiritual practices allows you to experience that.

3

Prayer is a Tool, Not a Crutch

Prayer is one of several spiritual tools available for the Satanist to use. Prayer is not a substitute for action, however. While prayer has its uses as a spiritual tool, it should not be your final act in trying to obtain what you want. Prayer should be supplementary, allowing for spiritual guidance on the path that you create.

Prayer without action is empty, and it does not produce the same results as doing something about your situation instead. For instance, if you pray for money yet do nothing outside of prayer to obtain it, you are not helping your situation. Prayer might give you the courage, insight, or focus so that you can take action.

Don't use prayer as a crutch. Use it instead as part of your overall strategy. You should do everything you can to help yourself and use prayer as guidance and as a way to seize upon opportunity. You can't expect to win if you don't play the game.

If you want to succeed, then go after it! Prayer should be combined with action to achieve the best results possible. Satan helps those that help themselves.

The left hand path teaches us to be self-sufficient. This means that we can't just sit back and expect Satan and other demons to work miracles for us. While you can ask for assistance through prayer, and there are some incredible things that can happen, there are still things that you will have to accomplish on your own. Satan may show you the road, but the road ahead is yours to walk.

As a form of theurgic magic, prayer reaches out to deities and recruits their assistance for your needs. But, just like magic, their abilities are limited according to the obstacles in your way. Prayer works because it opens the door to possibility, and while anything is possible not everything is likely. Approaching Satanic prayer as a means to an end instead of simply as a solution is a wise choice.

Many of you may have come from a Christian background where they teach that prayer leaves your fate in your god's hands. So all you have to do is just pray and wait. It is a method of inaction where you wait for results.

However, with Satanic prayer, when you are working with the forces of Satan, you are working with the forces of action instead. You are not complacent – you are focused. You are not at the mercy of fate – you are instead taking action and directing your own life. Satanic prayer gives you the opportunity to do these things for yourself.

4

Respecting The Forces of Darkness

Why you use prayer is just as important as how you chose to pray. Mostly when we think of praying, it reminds us of holding the hands together while praying. Some pray with the hands clasped together at the palms, and others find more comfort in praying with the hands folded.

Respecting The Forces Of Darkness

Some believe that folded hand praying was adopted by Christians through the practice of Judaism.[1] However, the practice of folded hand praying has been found in many cultures around the world. In general, the folded hand position shows respect, obedience, and submission.

While you may be familiar with the Christian way of praying, Satanists can also have their own way of praying as well. My suggestions include the use of the sign of the horns, with the left hand held over the heart. As an alternative, both hands can be held together with the sign of the horns. This hand gesture is made by extending the index and little finger while holding the middle and ring finger down with the thumb. It is commonly known as the 'sign of the horns'.

Many cultures around the world have used this hand gesture to cast out negative forces. In the eastern spiritual practices of Buddhism this similar hand sign, called the *Karana mudra* is used to cast out negativity.[2]

A similar hand sign also made its way to the west, in European and Mediterranean culture, as a charm and a hand gesture. It served as a way to emulate the horned head of an animal, in order to ward off the 'evil eye'.[3]

Western magic had adopted this same hand sign too for a similar purpose. In the practices of paganism and Wicca the hand sign is used to signify the horned god, Cernunnos, or Pan. [4]

Where the horned hand intersects with Satanism seems to have started with the popular culture of rock and roll. Some believe that the first use of this hand sign came through music artists who used it to signify various things. Most popularly, it was used by the band Coven on the back of their 1969 debut album, "Witchcraft Destroys Minds and Reaps Souls". [5]

The tradition seemed to have caught on with many other rock bands throughout the years. Many stars and public figures use the sign of the horns just to represent something that is awesome or fun. The sign of the horns became as ubiquitous as the peace sign.

But, like many things in Satanism, including the goat and the pentagram, the symbolism of the horned hand became co-opted early on by public figures in Satanism to represent a Satanic hand gesture. When used in prayer, worship and devotion it is a hailing to the infernal forces of Satan. This gives the Satanist a feeling of sincerity, devotion and self-empowerment. In the end, do what feels natural for you so that you can focus on the overall feeling of your prayer instead.

How you choose to end a prayer is an important consideration as well. Christians may end their prayer with "amen", which acts as a final ending or affirmation for the prayer. The word "amen", found in Christianity, Judaism and Islam has its roots in several languages, but it was through Judaism that the word was translated and handed down through our modern age.[6]

A prayer should have an ending so it feels complete and final. Many Satanists would not feel comfortable ending a prayer with "amen", so it is my suggestion that you may end your prayers with the simple "so it is done", instead.

5

The Spirit of Satan

Who or what is Satan? Throughout time people have tried to put a name and an image on dark and destructive forces in the world. Satan represents many things to many people. But for Satanists, we feel that Satan is a motivating force that allows us to live life the way that we want. Satan provides to us knowledge and self empowerment. With Satan, we are free from the bonds of sin and can live the way how we are meant to live.

Many Satanists feel that Satanism is a focus on the material world, and because of this, Satan personifies the natural world and nature. With Satanism, we realize our animal nature, and as creatures living in the natural world that we exist in. We are encouraged to seek out and understand our own human nature, instead of denying it or feeling guilty for who or what we are.

I won't say that Satanism is ancient or that Satan is an ancient god – but Satan personifies something special for us in our modern age, something that is timeless. Darkness is all that was in the beginning, and it will be all that is left in the end. And the Satanist lives for the here and now, enjoying the things that life and the material world has to offer.

So, what does Satan represent to you? Because spirituality is a personal journey, you have to find out on your own. Satan could be a force or energy, directing your life. Satan could be a god that you worship, or a devil that you make a pact with. Or, Satan can be a friend and ally, a motivating force. Take the time to learn about Satan's realm to develop your own personal understanding of Satan – the spirit of the black flame.

6

Satanic Prayers

This series of simple prayers was created by me, some of them based on a Christian formula such as the Lord's prayer and the Prayer for Satan's Kingdom. These Satanic prayers offer you a structured way of praying based on familiarity, and to provide to you infernal inspiration.

Satanic Prayers

AS BELOW, SO ABOVE...

7

A Backwards Blessing

The first time that I encountered the Lord's Prayer in reverse was in the mid-90s, from a book called "Mastering Witchcraft" by the occult author Paul Huson.[7] He claimed that saying this prayer was the first step to becoming a witch, as if it would act as an initiation for a new witch. Huson's rite included candle burning, and saying the prayer on three consecutive nights. While reciting the prayer in reverse, the initiate is made to feel and visualize the chains and bonds of Christianity being broken.

The original Lord's Prayer was made centuries ago, but in the 1800s, one author decided to put his own spin on it. The artist and poet William Blake went as far as writing a unique Satanic-inspired version of the Lord's Prayer based on the original.

Blake believed that reading the Lord's Prayer in reverse was an invocation to Satan, saying: "This is Saying the Lords Prayer Backwards which they say Raises the Devil". Blake's version was a hailing of Satanic forces and even went as far to proclaim that the Christian god should instead, have worshiped man. [8]

SPIRITUAL SATANIST PRAYER BOOK

The Lord's prayer can be found in the mythology of the Christian Bible, in Luke and Matthew. The prayer's intention is a story to illustrate the correct way to pray to the Christian god. The most common and widely used variant of this prayer originates from the 1928 Prayer Book of the Episcopal Church.[9]

Many Satanists come from a Christian background, so a prayer like this may enable them to let go of the bonds that once held them back. Saying the Lord's Prayer backwards seems blasphemous, but in a way it is also a means to undo or reverse one's previous ties with Christianity. This prayer can be said before a ritual, and is especially useful for those who are using this prayer as part of an initiation rite or a personal black mass.

A Backwards Blessing

Here are two versions of the prayer, an easier to pronounce phonetic version, and the actual Episcopal prayer in reverse.

LORDS PRAYER IN REVERSE
ALSO KNOWN AS A BACKWARDS BLESSING
PHONETIC PRAYER:

Nema! Livee morf su revilled tub
Noishaytpment ootni ton suh deel
Suh tshaiga sapsert tath yeth
Vigrawf eu za sespsert rua suh vigrawf.
Derb ilaid rua yed sith suh vig
Neveh ni si az thre ni
Nud eeb liw eyth
Muck mod-ngik eyth
Main eyth eeb dwohlah
Neveh ni tra chioo
Rertharf rua!

SPIRITUAL SATANIST PRAYER BOOK

BACKWARDS BLESSING, ORIGINAL VERSION:
nemA!
reve dna reve rof
yrolg eht dna rewop eht dna
modgnik eht si eniht roF
live morf su reviled tub
noitatpmet otni ton su dael dna
su tsniaga ssapsert ohw esoht evigrof ew
sa
sessapsert ruo su evigrof dna
daerb yliad ruo yad siht su eviG
nevaeh ni si ti sa htrae no
enod eb lliw yhT
emoc modgnik yhT
eman yht eb dewollaH
nevaeh ni tra ohw rehtaF ruO

A Backwards Blessing

8

Satan's Prayer

Satanists have their own version of the Lord's Prayer. Shared for many years, it is a Satanic interpretation of the Lord's Prayer, made for the praise of the earthly kingdom of Satan. While it's origins are not known, it has been passed down to Satanists throughout the decades.

Satan's Prayer

In fact, in 1991, the Church of Satan member's band, Acheron, recorded their own version of this prayer as a song on their Rites of the Black Mass metal album.[10] Titled, *"The Prayer of Hell"*, these verses are a perfect compliment to use just before a ritual begins.

The prayer below is the common variant of Satan's Prayer known to many Satanists.

SATAN'S PRAYER
Our Father
Who art in Hell
Cursed be thy name
Thy kingdom upon earth has come
Thy will be done in hell as it is on earth
Grant us your power and might
And lead us into temptation

SPIRITUAL SATANIST PRAYER BOOK

Deliver us unto evil
Thine is the kingdom of earth
The power and the glory
Forever and ever
So it is done!

9

A Satanic Blessing

This Satanic blessing calls upon the benefits of Satan and three other demons to strengthen you. This is a prayer that you can use for focus and direction and it calls upon each demon to help you in beneficial ways.

In calling upon Satan you are asking to strengthen what is closest to you in the

A Satanic Blessing

material world. In calling upon Lucifer, you are asking for knowledge and wisdom. In praying to Belial, you are asking for the way to be open. And lastly, in calling to Lilith, you are asking for creative forces in your life.

SATANIC BLESSING

Satan, bless my home, bring peace and safety to my house and my family
Satan, bless my loved ones with happiness and keep them from harm
Satan, bless my life with success and fulfillment, help me to seek my purpose

Lucifer, bless my spirit with the knowledge of your love
Lucifer, bless my mind so that I may see truth in all that I seek

Lucifer, bless my intellect and knowing so that I may know illumination

Belial, bless my will to enable me to succeed
Belial, bless my situations so that the path may be open and clear
Belial, bless my inner strength so that I may have direction

Lilith, bless my creations so that they may grow strong
Lilith, bless my intuition and knowing so that I may be sure
Lilith, bless my heart so that it may be open to self-love
So it is done!

10

Laude Satanas

This prayer is in praise of Satan as the ruler of the material world. I felt that a book on prayers to Satan wouldn't be complete without a Satanic prayer translated in Latin. So, below, is two renditions of this prayer – one in English, and the second version translated to Latin. A prayer like this may be useful in your ritual work as an opening.

Laude Satanas

PRAISE SATAN

Praise Satan, Praise Satan, Praise Satan
In the name of Satan's black flame
Power to the children of the earth.
The great king, we glorify you and join
in adoration of your might
Satan, the master of realms below
On our earth Satan rules the material
and strong
With glory and power forever
So it is done!

SPIRITUAL SATANIST PRAYER BOOK

LAUDE SATANAS, LATIN TRANSLATION
Sit laus Satanas: laudate Satanas: laudate Satanas.
Satanas in nomine nigra flamma.
Potestatem filios terrae.
Et rex magnus, glorificamus te iungere
Tantum ergo Sacramentum Veneremur virtutis tuae satanas,
Dominum nostrum de terra deorsum regionum
Satan regit et fortis materia, et gloria, et imperium sempiternum
Sic factum est!

Laude Satanas

11

The Infernal Trinity

The Infernal trinity is a prayer that opens the gateway to chthonic realms. Here we have the elements of earth (as Satan), air (as Lucifer) and water (as Lilith) combining to complete the fourth manifestation of fire (as Belial). With this formula, the gate or path is opened with the final demon, Belial.

The Infernal Trinity

We have the body, as seen in Satan, the mind as seen in Lucifer, the heart as seen in Lilith, and finally the spirit, as seen in Belial.

THE INFERNAL TRINITY
Glory unto Satan, Ruler of the Earth!
Who by his infernal powers keeps me in his favor
Return me to the spirit of the animal and the earth
My body is your body

Glory unto Lucifer, Ruler of the Air
Who by his illumination delivered me from ignorance
And opened for me the way of knowledge
My mind is your mind

Glory unto Lilith, Ruler of the Waters

Who has blessed me with her creation
By her graces I receive daily from her fertile womb
My heart is your heart

Glory unto the three Infernal deities
Who enable me to manifest my will
Through the black flame and the gateway of Belial
Now and forever,
So it is done!

The Infernal Trinity

12

In Praise of Satan's Kingdom

Satan's Kingdom is our material and earthly realm, and the four demons that preside within it represent the four directions and the four elements. This simple prayer evokes these four spiritual beings and aims to praise Satan's kingdom for all of its infernal glory!

In Praise Of Satan's Kingdom

PRAYER FOR THE PRAISE OF SATAN'S KINGDOM
Praise, Hail Satan!
Glory be to Satan the Father of the Earth
And to Lucifer, our guiding light
And to Lilith, the Mother of the night
And to Belial who walks between worlds
As it was in the void of the beginning
Is now, and ever shall be,
Satan's kingdom without end
So it is done!

13

The Satanist's Creed

The Satanist's Creed is a prayer that you can use for devotion or praise for Satan. This prayer seeks to establish your favor with Satan, Lucifer and Lilith.

This prayer is a declaration of your faith and devotion to Satan. This simple prayer can also be said after you complete a personal pact with Satan, to

The Satanist's Creed

affirm your relationship with Satan, and to seal the deal.

This prayer was modeled after one of the oldest Christian prayers. It was created in 325 A.D. at a time when Rome was converting from it's state religion.

Its aim was to unify the varied groups of Christians at the time under one creed.[11] Called the Nicene creed, it was created as a declaration of one's faith.

This Satanist version of the creed provides to you your own declaration of your personal allegiance to Satan.

SPIRITUAL SATANIST PRAYER BOOK

SATANIST'S CREED

I believe in the force of Satan
The source of the void
Ruler of the earth king of the world,
And in Lucifer, the guiding light and
the morning star above.
And Lilith, who seeded the world with
her creation
I believe I am my own church
I hold the spirit of Satan within my
heart;
I was born without the stain of sin
my spirit is one with Satan
As it is now and ever will be,
So it is done!

The Satanist's Creed

14

Prayer of Satan's Powers

Use this prayer in your time of need, to seek reassurance or to reach out to the spirit of Satan. This prayer can help you to focus on your goals and allow you to center your being. With this prayer you are asking Satan to help you to help yourself. Satan can only help you to realize the power and strength that lives within you, after all.

Prayer Of Satan's Powers

THE PRAYER OF SATAN'S POWERS

Satan, grant me the power to be strong in spirit
Grant me the ability to see what is right for me
Grant me the wisdom to understand your ways
Grant me the knowledge to empower myself

Power in the name of Satan to break the bonds that hold me back
Power in the name of Satan to overcome my weaknesses

SPIRITUAL SATANIST PRAYER BOOK

Power in the name of Satan to be strong within

Grant me the ability to know what is right for me
Grant me the vision to have knowledge in your ways
I accept your guidance and wisdom
In the name of Satan
So it is done!

15

Prayer of Satan's Riches

It is said that Satan is the ruler of the material world. The author of Demonology and Devils states: *"For a long time every successive discovery of science, every invention of material benefit to man, was believed by priest-ridden peoples to have been secured by compact with the devil."* [12] The material benefits that

Prayer Of Satan's Riches

humans created and enjoyed in life belong to the infernal kingdom.

Satan is the god of the material world, so why not ask for assistance? This prayer is especially helpful when combined with the use of magic, and it can be said during the casting of money spells.

PRAYER OF SATAN'S RICHES
Satan thank you for the riches you have brought to me
Bring me victory in my desire to grow in riches
O, Satan, ruler of the material world
Bring your abundance and mercy
Grant me that which I desire
Fill me with your power and spirit
So it is done!

16

Baphomet, The Source Of Creation

The Baphomet is a central figure in Satanism, symbolic of many of the things that Satanism represents. The goat was first recognized as Azazel, the scapegoat of the Jewish people when they set it free in the wilderness, carrying the sins of the people. Later on in history, blame fell on the Knights Templar for the worship of Baphomet.

The Baphomet was the creature that the occultist Eliphas Levi used to represent the spirit of initiation. What does this "initiation" mean? According to Levi, the Baphomet was symbolic of the void and the creation that comes from it. Simply meaning, that the Baphomet is the initiation or beginning from where all things emanate.

The Baphomet brings us to the source and the beginning of creation, the void from which all things originate. And it is the same symbol that Satanists adopted as their own years later, through the pentagram and the goat.[13]

SPIRITUAL SATANIST PRAYER BOOK

PRAYER TO BAPHOMET
I call upon Baphomet!
Father of Wisdom,
Mother of Truth and Lie,
Bringer of Day and Night!
Gather and dissolve your Silent wisdom among us!
As we look inside we will know,
As within so Without,
As above, So below!
So it is done!

Baphomet, The Source Of Creation

17

Lucifer, The Bringer Of Enlightenment

Lucifer, the ancient Roman god of the morning star – he brings to us enlightenment, and the dawning of knowledge! Lucifer's history has been entwined with Satan for many centuries. Originally the Greek god known as Phosphorous, Lucifer was adapted by the Romans.

Lucifer, The Bringer Of Enlightenment

Lucifer shares his ancient legends with Venus, where she was recognized not only as a goddess but also as a planet and a star. Both the morning and evening stars were recognized as separate entities, the ancient Greeks naming them Eosphorus for the morning star and Hesperus for the evening star.[14]

The Roman Latin name, Lucifer means 'lux' (light) and 'ferre', (to bear). In the mythology of the Christian bible, in the book of Isaiah, Lucifer is named as 'the morning star'. Within the book of Isaiah, the fall of Lucifer is an allegory for the destruction of Babylon's king, Helel ben Shahar.[15]

The dual male-female nature of Lucifer, is portrayed as both a god of beauty and a god of wisdom. Through Lucifer, the animal nature of the human spirit is transmuted into an intelligent being through knowledge and wisdom.

After the advent of Christianity as a state religion, however, the morning star began to symbolize an era of Roman gods that eventually was erased from history.

Versions of the Bible that are available do not explicitly state that Satan is the same as Lucifer. However, throughout time, the effect of monotheism reduced all former gods into demons. These demons were assimilated into Satan through literary works outside of the Bible through apocrypha, stories and plays.

For instance, it wasn't until the publishing of books like Paradise Lost in the 1600s that society began to equate Lucifer with Satan.[16] In the story of Paradise Lost, Lucifer acted with independence. For this he was 'cast' to the earth along with all of the other demons, devils and gods into Pandemonium.

Lucifer then gathered his armies, and with Satan and Belial at his side he declared independence for all who would follow his example.

IN PRAISE OF LUCIFER

Lucifer, the light of dawn, the bringer of knowledge
Born from the east wind of the mother of morning
from coal to diamond your wisdom is known
as your star shines above, so it is below
Bring me understanding, prince of the air
Through the shining of your eternal black flame
So it is done!

Lucifer, The Bringer Of Enlightenment

18

Lilith, The Queen Of The Night

Lilith, she is the dark queen of the night! The mysterious power of woman is both respected and feared where ancient people believed that this spirit would not only give life but take it as well.

Ancient Babylonians feared her both as a goddess and as a demon. People said charms and prayers against Lilith to protect children from her in the night. In her legends spanning thousands of years, Lilith rules the oceans as a mother and creator, and similarly, as the winged predator beasts of the desert as a force of destruction.

When her legends migrated into Judaism she became the first wife of Adam. She refused to submit to her husband's will, and so she escapes to the Red Sea.[17] This is an allusion to a woman's monthly cycle, where even in ancient times it was misunderstood and demonized as something evil.

Lilith joined in sexual union with Samael who she took as a lover. It is there at the Red Sea that she is given her first form, where she spent her time giving birth to hoards of demons every night as punishment.

Lilith rules the realm of emotion and the element of water. She also represents all things of the night including the moon, and her sacred hunter bird, the owl.

The English versions of the Bible translated her name as 'screech-owl'. The original Hebrew Torah calls her by name, however:

"But there the Lilith rests and has found her resting place, there the owl has made its nest and she has laid eggs and hatched then and gathered its young under its shadow, but there have the vultures gathered, each one to her friend." [18]

Her form in the desert is an expression of the second form of Lilith – that of a barren goddess.

The prayer of Lilith's blessing calls upon her creative forces to help you to manifest your own spiritual influence into this world.

SPIRITUAL SATANIST PRAYER BOOK

LILITH'S BLESSING

Hail Lilith, full of darkness,
Demon Queen of the Night
Samael is with thee
Keeper of life and death
Blessed are thou among women
Blessed is the fruit of thy womb, the
demons of the night
Infernal lunar mother of darkness
Keep us under the shadow of your wing,
and upon our passing
So it is done!

Lilith, The Queen Of The Night

19

Belial's Blessing

Belial is the keeper of the infernal Gate. Belial is represented in the Cabala as the force opposite from divine creation. *"In opposition to the supreme emanation of light, the Adam Kadmon, stands as opponent, the Adam Belial."*[19]

Whereas the forces of light represent creation and perfection the forces of darkness are chaotic and destructive. But, we must have both in able to manifest the physical world. As a demon, Belial is the gatekeeper, useful as a way to tear down obstacles that stand in your way.

While the name of Belial has a varied history, the most common belief is that his name was sourced from Hebrew, where it is translated as 'beli' (without) and 'ya'al' (value).[20] Belial's name is often mentioned in Jewish texts in reference to those who are without a master, those who are wicked or without worth.

The Goetia grimorie lists Belial as a king who was created after Lucifer, alluding to his nature of giving favors to kings and rulers, who appears as a dual headed angel with a roaring chariot of fire.[21]

In another grimorie from 1583, the Pseudomonarchia daemonum, Belial is a demon who provides favors for those that seek his aid.

> *"He taketh the forme of a beautifull angell, sitting in a firie chariot; he speaketh faire, he distributeth preferments of senatorship, and the favour of friends, and excellent familiars."* [22]

As the spirit of fire, Belial is the initiator, and the spirit of force, power, assertion and will. Tapping into this essence can only happen after one has experienced the darkness within, through Satan, self knowledge through Lucifer, and facing the divine feminine and the realm of emotion. It is through this gateway that Belial leads the initiate.

Belial's Blessing

While the spirit of Belial is often mentioned as something that leads people astray, it is this diversion from normal conventions that often lead us to new discoveries or open doorways.

Just like fire acts as a dual gateway to both destruction and creation, Belial is the spirit of manifestation and of fire, the manifestation of the black flame. After all, manifestation is only truly realized when you become your own master. This prayer to Belial opens the path and lets you focus on clearing what stands in your way so that the way may be opened.

BELIAL'S BLESSING

Belial keeper of the infernal gates
Open the way and manifest my desires
Make way the path clear unto me
Burn that which stands in my way
Be the spark that lights the black flame
Renew my spirit and my will
As below, so above,
In Belial's name
So it is done!

Belial's Blessing

20

Infernal Reflections

Infernal Reflections

"Where thou has need, to arm my heart with strength..."

Inferno, Canto 34

21

Hymn To Satan

Giosuè Carducci was an influential poet, philosopher and politician from Pisa, Italy. His numerous works included the 1865 poem, *Inno A Satana* – a tribute to the force of Satan. Some say that Carducci was a "notorious praiser of Satan", perhaps because of his open and inventive expression and modernist ideas. [23]

Hymn To Satan

His poem, *Inno a Satana* remains one of the most famous poems about Satan, that not only praises Satan for his virtues but does not condemn Satan for his choice to be cast out of heavenly realms. Satan is invoked in this poem as the host of all that is good and pleasurable in the material world.

Satan is found in the beauty and pleasure of life. This poem is a reminder that Satan and the gods of old had been, and should be, celebrated for the things that make life good and worth living. Enjoy this beautiful work of poetry in praise of Satan!

SPIRITUAL SATANIST PRAYER BOOK

INNO A SATANA

To you, creation's
mighty principle,
matter and spirit
reason and sense

Whilst the wine
sparkles in cups
like the soul
in the eye

Whilst earth and
sun exchange
their smiles and
words of love

And shudders
from their secret embrace run down
from the mountains, and
the plain throbs with new life

To you my daring

Hymn To Satan

verses are unleashed,
you I invoke, O Satan
monarch of the feast.

Put aside your sprinkler,
priest, and your litanies!
No, priest, Satan
does not retreat!

Behold! Rust
erodes the mystic
sword of Michael
and the faithful

Archangel, deplumed,
drops into the void.
The thunderbolt lies frozen
in Jove's hand

Like pale meteors,

SPIRITUAL SATANIST PRAYER BOOK

spent worlds,
the angels drop
from the firmament

In unsleeping
matter,
king of phenomena,
monarch of form,

Satan alone lives.
He holds sway in
the tremulous flash
of some dark eye,

Or the eye which languidly
turns and resists,
or which, bright and moist,
provokes, insists.

He shines in the bright

Hymn To Satan

blood of grapes,
by which transient
joy persists,

Which restores fleeting
life, keeps
grief at bay,
and inspires us with love

You breathe, O Satan
in my verses,
when from my heart explodes
a challenge to the god

Of wicked pontiffs,
bloody kings;
and like lightning you
shock men's minds.

Sculpture, painting

SPIRITUAL SATANIST PRAYER BOOK

and poetry
first lived for you, Ahriman,
Adonis and Astarte,

When Venus
Anadyomene
blessed the
clear Ionian skies

For you the trees of
Lebannon shook,
resurrected lover
of the holy Cyprian:

For you wild dances were done
and choruses swelled
for you virgins offered
their spotless love,

Amongst the perfumed
palms of Idumea

Hymn To Satan

where the Cyprian
seas foam.

To what avail did
the barbarous Christian
fury of agape,
in obscene ritual,

With holy torch
burn down your temples,
scattering their
Greek statuary?

You, a refugee,
the mindful people
welcomed into their homes
amongst their household gods

Thereafter filling the throbbing
female heart

SPIRITUAL SATANIST PRAYER BOOK

with your fervor
as both god and lover

You inspired the witch,
pallid from endless enquiry,
to succor
suffering nature

You, to the intent gaze
of the alchemist,
and to the skeptical eye
of the sorcerer,

You revealed bright
new heavens
beyond the confines
of the drowsy cloister.

Fleeing from material
things, where you reside,

Hymn To Satan

the dreary monk took refuge
in the Theban desert.

To you O soul
with your sprig severed,
Satan is benign:
he gives you your Heloise.

You mortify yourself to no purpose,
in your rough sackcloth:
Satan still murmurs to you
lines from Maro and Flaccus

Amidst the dirge
and wailing of the Psalms;
and he brings to your side
the divine shapes,

Roseate amidst that
horrid black crowd,

SPIRITUAL SATANIST PRAYER BOOK

of Lycoris
and Glycera

But other shapes
from a more glorious age
fitfully fill
the sleepless cell.

Satan, from pages
in Livy, conjures fervent
tribunes, consuls,
restless throngs;

And he thrusts you,
O monk, with your memories
of Italy's proud past
upon the Capitol.

Hymn To Satan

And you whom the raging
pyre could not destroy,
voices of destiny,
Wycliffe and Huss,

You lift to the winds
your waning cry:
'The new age is dawning,
the time has come'.

And already mitres
and crowns tremble:
from the cloister
rebellion rumbles

Preaching defiance
in the voice of the
cassocked Girolamo
Savonarola

SPIRITUAL SATANIST PRAYER BOOK

As Martin Luther
threw off his monkish robes,
so throw off your shackles,
O mind of man,

And crowned with flame,
shoot lightning and thunder;
Matter, arise;
Satan has won.

Both beautiful and awful
a monster is unleashed
it scours the oceans
is scours the land

Glittering and belching smoke
like a volcano,
it conquers the hills
it devours the plains.

Hymn To Satan

It flies over chasms,
then burrows
into unknown caverns
along deepest paths;

To re-emerge, unconquerable
from shore to shore
it bellows out
like a whirlwind,

Like a whirlwind
it spews its breath:
'It is Satan, you peoples,
Great Satan passes by'.

He passes by, bringing blessing
from place to place,

SPIRITUAL SATANIST PRAYER BOOK

upon his unstoppable
chariot of fire

Hail, O Satan
O rebellion,
O you avenging force
of human reason!

Let holy incense
and prayers rise to you!
You have utterly vanquished
the Jehova of the Priests.

Hymn To Satan

22

Lucifer in Starlight

Lucifer in Starlight is a beautiful poem that takes us through Lucifer's realm as the morning and evening star. It was authored by George Meredith, a Victorian era poet and author. Meredith often focused on social issues and psychological perspective in his works.

Written in 1883, *Lucifer in Starlight* is a

focus on the ethereal being of Lucifer as the morning and evening star, watching over the world.[24] Lucifer's fate, however, is to always remain within the realm of darkness, as Lucifer shines as just at the dawn and just before dusk.

In this poem, Lucifer is also portrayed as a fallen god when he is named as a prince, but then later on he is labeled as a fiend. His 'revolt from awe' is the shower of light that banishes the sight of the stars from the sky.

While the Christian might see this poem as a look at what Lucifer lost as he travels over the world, the Satanist knows that quite the opposite is true.

We recognize Satan is the god of this world. Lucifer provides the guiding light over Satan's dark kingdom and instead, is a shining herald for Satan's realm. Let this poem take you on Lucifer's journey.

LUCIFER IN STARLIGHT

On a starred night Prince Lucifer uprose,
Tired of his dark dominion, swung the fiend
Above the rolling ball, in cloud part screened,
Where sinners hugged their specter of repose.

Poor prey to his hot fit of pride were those.

And now upon his western wing he leaned,

Lucifer In Starlight

Now his huge bulk o'er Afric's sands careened,
Now the black planet shadowed Arctic snows.

Soaring through wider zones that pricked his scars
With memory of the old revolt from Awe,
He reached a middle height, and at the stars,
Which are the brain of heaven, he looked, and sank.

Around the ancient track marched, rank on rank,
The army of unalterable law.

SPIRITUAL SATANIST PRAYER BOOK

23

The Lady Lilith

Dante Gabriel Rosetti was a famous author, poet and painter who lived in the Victorian era. One of his most beautiful and memorable works is his painting of Lady Lilith.

Painted over a series of eight years, this beautiful work of art was sketched and painted after two women who both

The Lady Lilith

posed for him as models. The artist's intention was to give a modern look to the ancient legends of Lilith.[25]

Lady Lilith is shown with her long flowing hair, in an enchanting image of wild abandon. While she is seated indoors, behind her is a mirror which reflects a garden scene.

The sonnet for Lilith was modeled after Goethe's Lilith, and it is inscribed in the lower part of the painting's frame.

LADY LILITH

Of Adam's first wife, Lilith, it is told
(The witch he loved before the gift of Eve,)
That, ere the snake's, her sweet tongue could deceive,
And her enchanted hair was the first gold.

And still she sits, young while the earth is old,
And, subtly of herself contemplative,
Draws men to watch the bright web she can weave,
Till heart and body and life are in its hold.

The rose and poppy are her flowers; for where
Is he not found, O Lilith, whom shed scent

The Lady Lilith

And soft-shed kisses and soft sleep shall snare?

Lo! as that youth's eyes burned at thine, so went
Thy spell through him, and left his straight neck bent
And round his heart one strangling golden hair.

SPIRITUAL SATANIST PRAYER BOOK

Bibliography & Notes

1. Ausubel, Nathan. *The book of Jewish knowledge: an encyclopedia of Judaism and the Jewish people, covering all elements of Jewish life from biblical times to the present.* Crown Publishers, 1979. p. 351 Jewish origins of hand position while praying

2. Marotta, Janetti. "Karana Mudra." *Mudras*, 26 May 2014, janettimarotta.com/

karana-mudra/. "The Karana mudra is the gesture of warding off evil. This mudra emanates energy to rid such obstacles as sickness or negative thoughts."

3. catherine yronwode. "The Mano Cornuto, The Horned Hand" *Lucky Mojo Curio Co.* 1994, http://www.luckymojo.com/manocornuto.html. "The mano cornuto is an Italian amulet of ancient origin..The reference is to the horned head of an animal."

4. Cunningham, S. (2015). *Wicca: A Guide for the Solitary Practitioner*. Llewellyn Publications. p. 42 "Both have long been used to avert the evil eye and negativity, and the latter is used in Wicca, with points up, to represent the God in his horned aspect."

5. Coven. (1969). *Witchcraft Destroys Minds & Reaps Souls* [Vinyl recording]. Bill Traut.

6. *The Catholic Encyclopedia*. (1912). New York: Appleton. History of the word "Amen".

7. Huson, Paul. (1970). *Mastering Witchcraft*. Putnam. Lord's Prayer in Reverse

8. Paley, M. D. (2007). *Traveller in the Evening: The Last Works of William Blake*. Oxford University Press. p. 295 William Blake added his own notes to this writing in the margins of R.J. Thorton's book (*The Lords Prayer, Newly Translated from the original Greek*), paraphrasing the prayer as a praise to Satan, claiming that God was instead, a servant to man!

9. *The Book of Common Prayer*. (1958). Oxford University Press.

10. Prayer of Hell. (1991). On *Rites of the Black Mass* [Vinyl recording]. JL America.

11. "The Nicene Creed and its origins." *Catholic News Herald*, catholicnewsherald.com/faith/101-news/faith/364-the-nicene-creed-and-its-origins.

12. Conway, M. D. (2015). *Demonology and Devil-Lore*. S.l.: Forgotten Books. (Originally published in 1879) Source: p. 285

13. Satanas, Venus. "The Origin of the Baphomet, or Why Goats Are Satanic." *Spiritual Satanist*, Sept. 2017, www.spiritualsatanist.com/essays/satanism/baphomet-why-goats-are-satanic.html.

14. "Eosphoros & Hesperus." *Greek Gods of the Morning & Evening Stars*, www.theoi.com/Titan/AsterEosphoros.html.

15. Johnson, Dominique. "Everything About Lucifer in Ancient Mythology." *The Academician Theosophical*, 31 Jan. 2018, theacademiciantheosophical.wordpress.com/2015/06/30/everything-about-lucifer-in-ancient-mythology/.

16. Hancock, M. O. *Paradise lost / notes*. Coles, 1963. Ref. John Milton Paradise Lost, 1608

17. Gaines, Janet Howe. "Lilith, Seductress, heroine or murderer?" *Biblical Archaeology Society*, 91 Jan. 2017, www.biblicalarchaeology.org/daily/people-cultures-in-the-bible/people-in-the-bible/lilith/.

18. "Yeshayahu – Isaiah – Chapter 34." *Tanakh Online – Torah – Bible*, www.chabad.org/library/bible_cdo/aid/15965/jewish/Chapter-34.htm.

19. Metzger & Coogan. *Oxford Companion to the Bible*, 1993 p. 77.

20. Pick, Bernhard. *The Cabala: its influence on Judaism and Christianity*. Sun Books, 1993.

21. Crowley, Aleister. *The book of the Goetia or, The lesser key of Solomon the king: from numerous manuscripts in Hebrew, Latin, French and English*. The Occult Pub. House, 1903.

22. Weyer, Johann, et al. *Pseudomonarchia daemonum: illustrated English translation*. Abracax House, 2014.

23. "Giosuè Carducci – Biographical". *Nobelprize.org*. Nobel Media AB 2014. Web. 24 Feb 2018. http://www.nobelprize.org/nobel_prizes/literature/laureates/1906/carducci-bio.html

24. "Biography of George Meredith." *Poetry Foundation*, www.poetryfoundation.org/poets/george-meredith.

25. "Lady Lilith." *Rosetti Archive*, http://www.rossettiarchive.org/docs/s205.rap.html.

Image Credits

Cover: Pexels Stock Photos. Creative Commons.

Dedication Page, A Pact With Satan. *Compendium Maleficarum.* 1608.

p. 32 Artist Unknown. *Baphomet Drawing.* Clip Art Repository.

p. 38 Rops, Felicien. *Le Calvair Les Sataniques*. 1882. "The Satanic Calvary

Image Credits

(Cross)" from a series of 5 prints titled Les Satanics (The Satanics) A blasphemous scene with Satan upon the cross.

p. 50 Lawrence, Thomas. *Satan summoning his Legions*. 1797. Satan rises to power and summons his demonic legions.

p. 54 De Teramo, Jacobus. *Belial Before the Gates of Hell*. 1473. Belial opens the gates of Hell.

p. 60 *Osculum Infame*. 1608. Devotion is shown to Satan through the Devil's kiss, the 'kiss of shame'.

p. 70 Levi, Eliphas. *The Baphomet*. 1854. From his book, "Dogmas and Rituals of High Magic" Eliphas Levi illustrates the Baphomet, an anthropomorphic figure representing Satan.

p. 76 Fahrenkrog, Ludwig. *Lucifer Arising*. 1903. Lucifer rises in shining glory from the morning sky.

p. 82 Delville, Jean. *The Idol of Perversity*. 1891. The dangerous and fatal woman, as represented by Lilith.

p. 88 *Kings and Priests confer with Belial*. 1608. Belial acts as an intermediary or negotiator for Satan.

p. 90 Gustave Doré. 90 Canto 34 *Satan's Frozen Kingdom*. 1885. Infernal Reflections. Lucifer at the center of Hell, with a frozen reflection below him.

p. 106 Bromley, W. *Satan Risen from the Flood, Beelzebub Rising*. 1802. Satan rises up above the flood and calls to his armies below.

Image Credits

p. 111 Artist Unknown. *Engraving of Lucifer*. An androgynous representation of Lucifer, as the son of the morning, and the Venus star.

p. 117 Rosetti, Dante Gabriel. *Lady Lilith*. 1868. A Victorian depiction of womanly charm, a modern Lilith.

About The Author

My name is Venus Satanas. I've been a Satanist since 1992 and along the way, I have learned a lot about myself and the world around me through the path of Satanism.

I was fortunate when I was a child – I wasn't forced to be a Christian. I was allowed to explore a world that included the belief in energies and auras. My grandmother who raised me, had a library full of books on astrology. She taught me how to do money spells in the moonlight with silver coins. I spent my childhood reading as many books as I could. As a teenager, I took an interest in the world of art. It was my interest in art and history that lead me to find Satanism.

HOW I DISCOVERED SATANISM
In search of books on art history, I discovered Satanism at the local library in 1992, among the books in the reference section. The book was the Church of Satan written by Blanche Barton and Anton LaVey, the hardcover edition. This book offered a history of the Church of Satan and an idea of what Satanism was about. Satanism made

sense to me. For once, the world seemed right and the path of Satanism was something that empowered me.

During that time in America, in the late 90's, the Satanic Panic was slowly dying out. Being 13 at the time, I didn't really know about the panic and the hype surrounding Satanism, so I came to Satanism without expectations. I always had a spiritual view of Satan, though, and approached Satan as a god, equal in comparison to the Christian god. Satan was more than a symbol to me. I made my first personal pact with Satan that year in 1992, to initiate myself as a Satanist.

It wasn't until a few years later that I was finally able to read the Satanic Bible, at the age of 15. By then, I had developed

About The Author

my own independent way of practicing and living Satanism.

SATANIC OUTREACH

I started writing about Satanism in 2004, when I was at a time in my life when I was able to fully explore the world of the occult. There wasn't much online to help Satanists who had a spiritual view. Many of the resources out there were aimed at atheistic Satanists.

My biggest inspiration, though was Diane Vera and her Theistic Satanism website. I appreciated how she was able to present an objective view of Satanism while creating Satanism as part of a pantheistic religion. This was something new at the time and it contrasted with atheistic Satanism that was popular. And it made me happy to know that women were an important part of Satanism as well.

I understand the need for religious Satanism, but for me, I took a less religious approach. If Satanism is an expression of freedom, then why not be free from religious expression as well? I am a Spiritual Satanist, meaning that I have broken from the usual religious conventions in Satanism and created my own personal spiritual path and method of Satanic expression. I am also independent, meaning that I don't belong to any Satanic organizations or churches.

ABOUT MY WEBSITES
My website, SpiritualSatanist.com was an instant success. At my website, I offer

About The Author

instruction on independent, Spiritual Satanism, helping people from all around the world discover Satanism. In 2009, I created the supplemental Spiritual Satanist Blog to discuss reader's questions and to help others to understand the social issues that Satanists face today.

And along with this, I also created my own video channel on Youtube where I discuss Satanism, magic and the occult. In addition to this, I also run the Left Hand Path Books blog, a resource for Satanists to learn and discover the best books and authors in Satanism and the left hand path.

Despite my 'celebrity' status, I'm not interested in creating a group of followers. I want people to ask questions and to learn on their own. I think that those who are able to influence the future of Satanism shouldn't be telling people what to believe and how to act.

Historically, Satan is a figure of rebellion and so, why take the normal standard route of joining a group and being just a follower when you could learn to be a leader in your own right?

It is my hope that my *Spiritual Satanist Prayer Book: Infernal Reflections* can bring people closer to Satan, Lucifer, Belial and Lilith, and the left hand path.

Stay updated on all my latest projects: SpiritualSatanist.com and VenusSatanas.com!

www.ingramcontent.com/pod-product-compliance
Lightning Source LLC
Chambersburg PA
CBHW032041290426
44110CB00012B/898